The
Flower
in the
Pocket

Also in the **<u>be</u>ing human** series:

The Lost Sun

The Unwanted Friend

The Dragonfly in the Haze

For more information about the Being Human method, please refer to each book in the series. You will also find a video overview of the method via www.carriehayward.com/beinghuman. Further, you will find more information about the teachings in the list of resources provided at the end of this book.

The Flower in the Pocket

A **being human** guide to
finding growth through emotional pain

DR CARRIE HAYWARD

Illustrated by Elizabeth Szekely

EXISLE
PUBLISHING

First published 2023

Exisle Publishing Pty Ltd
PO Box 864, Chatswood, NSW 2057, Australia
226 High Street, Dunedin, 9016, New Zealand
www.exislepublishing.com

A CiP record for this book is available from the National Library of Australia.

ISBN 978-1-922539-89-2

Designed by Bee Creative
Typeset in Optima, 10.5pt
Printed in China

This book uses paper sourced under ISO 14001 guidelines from well-managed forests and other controlled sources.

10 9 8 7 6 5 4 3 2 1

Disclaimer

While this book is intended as a general information resource and all care has been taken in compiling the contents, neither the author nor the publisher and their distributors can be held responsible for any loss, claim or action that may arise from reliance on the information contained in this book. As each person and situation is unique, it is the responsibility of the reader to consult a qualified professional regarding their personal care.

For my mum —
her generous green thumb and
always flourishing heart.

Dr Carrie Hayward is a clinical psychologist who works with individuals to help them live more consciously and purposefully. Her training in Acceptance and Commitment Therapy (ACT) profoundly changed her approach to living, both professionally and personally.

Introduction

"

How rare and beautiful it truly is, that we exist.

—'Saturn', Sleeping At Last

Being human is truly remarkable. Our mere existence is beautiful, wondrous and mindbogglingly mysterious. But when it comes to the everyday and ordinary experience of being human, at times it can be really hard.

My years as a psychologist have taught me why — that is, the core reason as to why human beings are prone to psychological struggle. I believe this is one of the most important understandings I have learnt about the human condition.

You see, people come to see me, or any psychologist, with a vast range of struggles.

1

Some of us struggle with depressive states or anxiety issues. For others, it may be anger concerns, eating issues, or disharmony in our relationships, and so on. And these experiences are occurring on the background of our own histories and contexts.

It is therefore easy to forget that we are all from the same species, existing together on planet Earth — all trying to navigate life the best way we can. Given our internal world feels deeply private and isolated, we often assume that our psychology is different or abnormal — that there is something wrong with us — which can make us feel alone. Like we do not belong.

Yet despite our differences, all human beings share one of the greatest dilemmas of the human condition: our innate struggle with all the things we cannot control in our lives, including the hardships that happen around us and the emotional pain that happens inside us. And this is underpinned by a core function of our humanness: our survival response. This remarkable aspect of the human condition that keeps us alive can, paradoxically, work against us when we are experiencing hardship and pain. Our hardwired need for control can typically result in a disconnect with ourselves and our core values, which disrupts our way of being with ourselves, each other and the world. And it is when we are disconnected from our values — how we want to show up in the world — that we experience the greatest distress.

In short, our psychological struggle fundamentally occurs when our *humanness* disrupts our *beingness*.

I wrote the Being Human series to explore this dilemma of the human condition. The series is informed by Acceptance and Commitment Therapy (ACT) teachings, an evidence-based framework which helps us to develop psychological flexibility in order to live a mindful, values-based and purposeful life. Put simply, the essence of practising ACT is bringing awareness, and acceptance, to the 'human' in our experience, which allows us to bring choice and meaning to the 'being' in our moments. Allowing us to live our moments, and therefore our lives, as conscious and connected human beings.

> "
> *Pain is inevitable. Suffering is optional.*
> Haruki Murakami

The Being Human series features four stories that follow the journey of interconnected characters, illuminating the different ways we experience our shared struggle of the human condition. The stories are followed by an exploration into the teaching and conclude with a practical process for you to take into your life. Each book focuses on a different teaching, and therefore can stand alone, where you will learn one helpful process at a time.

This book in your hands — *The Flower in the Pocket* — focuses on how our hardwired struggle with emotional pain can, unwittingly, turn our pain into suffering. Through this story, you will learn about how we can change our relationship with emotional pain, to re-empower ourselves when dealing with situations that we cannot control.

Each book is one piece of the Being Human puzzle. The whole series — all books connected — forms the complete Being Human method.

By reading about the story of the characters in each book, you may see some of your own experience in their challenges. And hopefully, you will discover the power of awareness around your humanness, allowing you to engage with your values and have choice over your beingness, with yourself, others and the world. This is at the heart of our purpose and meaning as human beings.

And so, welcome aboard to Being Human. I hope you have an insightful and wondrous ride.

x Carrie

The story

Wilbur rubs his eyes as he walks out his front door. He smiles. The morning sun is spotlighting his garden; the creamy white gardenias greet him by swaying in the delicate breeze. He beams at the quiet.

Wilbur starts humming a catchy tune and crosses his lawn to the garden hose. The freshly mowed grass feels like soft carpet under his bare feet. He glances back over his shoulder and smiles at his two-storey white weatherboard cottage — pristine and orderly. Just the way Elizabeth, his late wife, always kept it.

He turns back to his garden, and from across the street Abigail, his long-standing neighbour, is waving at him. She is clutching the lilies that Wilbur left on her doorstep the previous evening. They light up her long face. He's been doing this every week since she became an empty nester. Wilbur smiles graciously and waves back.

Patrick, the vegan chef from down the street, will arrive for his fresh basil later in the day. Wilbur makes a mental note to make sure it is picked and waiting for him. Wilbur offers the produce from his garden to all his neighbours on Park Street.

He picks up the garden hose, his plants waiting eagerly for water, like cross-legged preschoolers expecting their mid-morning story. But first, he scans the contenders for resettlement to his kitchen vase. He picks the winner — a modest blue daisy from the back row of flowerbeds. Wilbur gently rubs his thumbs across the soft velvety petals, admiring the flower's unpretentious charm. He carefully places the daisy in the pocket of his pyjama top before turning on his hose and watering those left idle.

Suddenly a radio announcer's voice cuts through the quiet. 'Good morning listeners, thank you for joining us on this spectacular Saturday morning,' the voice blares from the open window over the fence. Wilbur's new neighbour is awake.

It has started already. He sighs.

When the neighbour moved in last month, Wilbur had fantasised about 'borrowed cups of sugar' and friendly chats over the fence. But this vision had quickly been dispelled.

Wilbur stifles a yawn, the aftermath of his broken sleep. He frowns as he mulls over the late-night barking from the neighbour's burly and boisterous dog.

And now the loud radio.

With rising frustration, he scans the neighbour's property for more evidence of disturbance. The overflowing rubbish bins, scattering waste onto their shared footpath. The decrepit Jeep parked outside Wilbur's house, marking its territory with oil stains on the bitumen. He feels the heat engulfing his chest.

A loud bark erupts behind him. He spins around to discover the neighbour's dog digging a large hole underneath their shared fence, scattering soil over Wilbur's manicured lawn.

'You scoundrel!' Wilbur screeches, flicking his gushing hose towards the dog. But the dog is too quick and escapes back through the newly dug trench into the safety of his own yard.

Wilbur is livid. He strides out of his gate and into his neighbour's property. The dog is now nowhere to be seen. Wilbur marches up to his neighbour's door, banging his fist, demanding confrontation. However, there is no response.

Storming back into his house, he bounds over to his desk and furiously scrawls a note. The wild flame in his chest cheers him along as his fury spills onto the paper. Once the note is written, Wilbur charges outside again and back to his new neighbour's property and thrusts the hostile note under the front door.

Wilbur struts back to his house, with his chest slightly puffed out. The flame is now tamed. But the embers of anger continue to smoulder and have morphed into a heavy pounding deep in his gut.

For the rest of the day, Wilbur keeps one eye on his front window, impatient to see evidence of his neighbour responding to the note. He struggles to concentrate on anything else. He tries reading his newspaper. But his eyes circle the same article, over and over, without comprehension. He tries taking a nap, but his mind is swimming, drowning rather, in a sea of self-righteous assumptions. Not even his usual Saturday afternoon pastime — the football on TV — can seduce his attention. His thoughts are too busy conspiring with his blazing chest, provoking each other with a shared agenda to prevail over his neighbour's injustice.

Later, Wilbur hears movement on his garden path and energy surges through his body in anticipation. However, he peers through the window to see that it's just Patrick, arriving for his basil. Wilbur's frustration escalates. He ignores the knock at the front door.

Early the next morning, Wilbur tosses and turns in bed. The barking has continued, although Wilbur can no longer distinguish between the rowdy howls from next door and the snarling thoughts about his neighbour circling his mind.

How dare they!

So selfish. Arrogant.

They're ruining my peace!

He drags himself out of bed and starts getting dressed. Suddenly, he is startled by a loud bang on his bedroom window. Wilbur stomps over and flings open the curtains. The weather appears to be mimicking his temper; darkened clouds now dominate the sky, and thunder begins to growl, a deep rumbling warning.

Through the window, he spots the source of the bang: his neighbour's newspaper, lying on the porch below. Wilbur charges downstairs and hauls open his front door. He snatches the paper from the ground and marches to his bin at the side of the house to discard it. Wilbur throws the newspaper in the bin then slams down the lid, to both punctuate and discharge his anger.

As he turns to walk back around to his front door, Wilbur suddenly stops in his tracks. He gasps at the backdrop of lifelessness surrounding him. The daisy blooms are limp and brown. The fern leaves are curled and wilted. The succulents are a ghostly grey. His precious garden has started to wither.

His heart now pounding, Wilbur rushes over to his garden beds. He picks a wilted gardenia bloom that shrivels in the cup of his hand. He examines the rest of his plants, an assemblage of dull limbs, all sagging downwards — as though each plant has turned away, in shame, from Wilbur's desperate gaze. Wilbur could feel the sensation of his heartbeat drop deep into his stomach, and then appear to fall to the wet ground below. He cannot comprehend how his thriving garden has suddenly lost its shimmer. As shock settles in, Wilbur turns to walk away. He cannot bear it. He trudges out through his front gate, escaping the dreary scene. Rain starts to

fall. He is still wearing his pyjama top but he does not notice.

In a stupor, Wilbur continues walking down the street, the rain spattering around him. He soon finds himself at the entrance to his local park. He walks through the entrance and heads down a winding path, allowing the crushed gravel track to take custody over the direction he moves in. It takes him through an open gate, walled by a tall, hedged fence.

His head hung low, Wilbur does not notice a young woman who is walking towards him. Passing by, the woman slips a large umbrella under Wilbur's arm. It takes a few

moments before Wilbur realizes. He then stops in his tracks, looks down at the umbrella and tries to make sense of it. Confused, he slowly turns back towards the young woman. But she has already walked off in the other direction.

Wilbur takes hold of the umbrella in his hands. His fingers find the small release button. As the canopy pops open, it appears to push away his sense of oblivion at the same time.

Now more alert, and armoured, Wilbur walks on. He continues along the pathway that circles the large pond. Up ahead, he sees a man pushing a small boy in a stroller, also heading towards the pond.

Wilbur watches as the man suddenly stops. He turns away from the stroller to start tapping on his phone. The child, evidently unbuckled, climbs out of his stroller to chase an autumn leaf soaring by. After a few moments the man looks up from his phone, but the child is no longer in view.

Wilbur watches as the man's face pales with fear while he frantically looks around. Wilbur is just about to call out to help when the little boy emerges from behind a tree. Wilbur notices the colour return to the man's face, transitioning to red. It appears that anger has sprouted from the man's fear. He begins to scold the child. Tears start to stream down the child's face. Within moments, the man's eyes

and posture soften. He lifts his arms to wrap them around the little boy — his love surfacing and pushing all other emotions aside.

The rain has now stopped. Wilbur reaches into his pocket to search for a tissue to wipe the wet from his brow. Instead, his fingers touch something else. He pulls out the blue daisy he picked from his garden the day before. Wilbur is surprised to see that it is still in his pocket. And it is still alive.

He stares at the graceful flower, its integrity untarnished by the rain. Wilbur feels, once again, the pounding deep below his stomach. His gut is speaking; devotion is there — a companion to the flame of anger that has been wavering above. He places his free hand over his chest. Now Wilbur can feel his love begin to push its way to the surface.

With the daisy in the palm of his hand, Wilbur decides to go home. As he heads towards the open gate, he spots the young woman across the other side of the pond. He places the umbrella against the gate, hoping it will find its way back to her.

Wilbur is now walking with more vigour, eager to arrive home. As he enters Park Street, he slows down as he approaches his neighbour's house. Barking loudly, the burly dog bounds up to the gate to greet him. Wilbur automatically flinches. But this time, as he opens the gate, he reaches down and pats the dog's belly. Wilbur notices the softness of its fur.

He begins walking up the neighbour's path, almost tripping over a protruding broken paver as he swerves around an abandoned dog toy. He can hear raucous music coming from inside the house. Wilbur feels the familiar flame reignite inside his chest. He hesitates for a few moments, then glances down at the daisy in his hand. He takes a deep breath. He chooses to keep walking, calmly, towards the front door. Wilbur decides not to knock; he will come back later to talk with his neighbour when he's dried and dressed. Instead, he places the daisy on his neighbour's doormat.

Heading back down the neighbour's path, Wilbur looks over their shared fence towards his garden. He is startled by what he sees. The daisies are parading their golden bellies and white manes. The ferns have blossomed a cheerful green. The yuccas are towering, their arms erect and noble. His garden has returned to life.

Wilbur shakes his head in wonder and smiles. He then keeps walking past the neighbour's dog, who is now lying peacefully on the uneven path. Finally, he reaches his gate. He walks through and makes sure to keep it open. He cannot take his eyes off his flourishing garden. So transfixed by its sprouting beauty, Wilbur does not notice that the loud music from next door has now ceased.

Humming his favourite tune, Wilbur walks over to one of his garden beds. He straightens a trampled fern and surveys his basil, shimmering with beads of rain left over from the previous downpour. He decides to pick an extra bunch for Patrick. He leans over to reach the basil. As he snaps off the stems, droplets of water fall to the earth below, sprinkling the ebbing flame inside his chest on their way down.

Afterword

Emotional pain is part of the human experience. Not only a natural response to life events that hurt, painful emotions also serve an evolutionary purpose: they encourage us to act in ways that improve our chances of survival and help us grow and develop as human beings.

For example, anger. Ranging from mild irritation to seething rage, anger is typically experienced when we face a perceived injustice or some form of loss. It provides a surge of energy and allows us to feel more in charge, rather than vulnerable or helpless. Essentially, anger offers us a sense of control and power — often illusory — in the context of vulnerability and uncertainty.

However, the character of anger is paradoxical. It can be the most powerful and the most disempowering of all the emotions we experience.

Anger and the paradox of control

The power of anger lies in its biological function. Physiologically, anger serves a protective purpose by triggering the fight mode of the 'fight, flight or freeze' survival system. The physiological fight response — involving sensations such as tightness in the chest and high body temperature — is very helpful because it primes the body for quick action when faced with life-threatening situations or perceived wrongdoings, whether from nature, other people, or events in the world.

The survival system bypasses the rational mind, automatically switching us into control mode. In this mode, the mind seeks to control our external environment and the internal physiological emotion, to attain a sense of safety. The control mode can be triggered even when our survival is not physically threatened.

In the presence of anger, the mind's control reaction may present overtly, through aggressive, violent or hostile behaviour. The mind's attempt to control can also take the form of combative and ruminating thoughts. Such thoughts may include assumptions, judgments and rigid narratives about the source and reason behind the perceived wrongdoing.

Our need for control is problematic given we do not have full, or direct, control over external situations or our physiological responses. Furthermore, our attempts to control paradoxically result in a loss of agency when our behaviour becomes governed by anger, including our internal behaviour — that is, our attention. Our attention can be hijacked by ruminating thoughts, which are linked to the anger response, about the situation or person. This preoccupation disempowers us, particularly when it takes on an addictive nature, and we can find ourselves looking around our environment to find things to be angry about.

Scratching the itch

Most of us have endured the discomfort of being bitten by a mosquito. In tropical climates especially, many of us can find ourselves peppered with the unwanted red spots left by a mosquito's thirsty bite. Once bitten, an itchy sensation usually results. And, often without realizing, we find ourselves reactively scratching the bite to control the uncomfortable feeling. Yet as we know, the relief is only temporary. Often fleeting. The bite becomes more inflamed by the scratching, and the short-lived relief is quickly followed by an even more intensified itch. What then happens? We experience the temptation to scratch again, even more feverously — we get caught in an unworkable and all-consuming struggle with trying to control the feeling.

Our innate control reaction to emotional 'itches' is just as problematic. Just like with a mosquito bite, our struggle against emotional discomfort, such as anger, can end up doing the opposite of what it is trying to achieve. All the attention and energy we are giving to the struggle can end up fuelling the feeling rather than eliminating it. We become overwhelmed by the emotion, simply from trying to control it. And further, our struggle can take our attention from everything else that is happening, and that matters to us, in that moment.

In the story, Wilbur's anger arose in reaction to his neighbour, whose actions were inconsistent with the calm and order that Wilbur valued. His fight reaction was activated. He incessantly struggled with the 'itch' of his anger and his attention became preoccupied with unrelenting thoughts and stories about the situation — his attempt to resolve the uncomfortable feeling. However, the more Wilbur failed to control, the more aggressive and distressed he became. And more destructively, his aggressive behaviours had taken his attention away from living his values, such as being a friendly neighbour.

Wilbur lost control as a result of trying to control. By struggling with his anger, he had unwittingly handed over control to the situation — and the person — he was desperately trying to change. This caused more suffering. And just like his cherished garden that began to wilt, Wilbur's connection to himself — his value system — deteriorated. Feelings of anguish and despair then dominated.

Therefore, the problem of emotional discomfort, such as anger, is not the felt experience of it. But rather, it's our struggle with it. That is, when our mind tries to fight the feeling and control the situation. This automatic struggle can dictate our behaviours and hijack our attention, disconnecting us from the person we want to be.

It is this disconnect that turns pain into suffering, a consequence which is twofold: individual suffering that comes from the struggle and disconnect; and larger-scale societal suffering when our control reactions lead to hostility and aggression against our fellow human beings.

The value in emotional pain

The presence of emotional discomfort simply tells us that something has happened that we perceive as going against what matters to us.

Emotional pain, such as anger, can therefore feel bad, but it is not 'bad' for it to be there. Instead, it tells us about the 'good' in what we care about — our values. And, more broadly, the human phenomenon of all emotional pain reminds us of the magnificence in the human capacity to care so deeply.

In the words of Professor Steven Hayes (co-founder of Acceptance and Commitment Therapy), 'we only hurt where we care'. Or rather, we only hurt because human beings have the capacity to care. And this is what makes life matter.

Accepting emotional discomfort

We rationally know that the only way for a mosquito bite to heal is to leave it alone. However, to stop ourselves from scratching it we need to be willing for the discomfort to be there. The itch will then dissipate in its own time. The same applies to emotions, including anger. The uncomfortable 'itch' of emotional pain will naturally shift only when we stop trying to control it. To do this, we need to accept its presence.

Accepting discomfort does not mean liking or resigning ourselves to the feeling. Nor does it mean approving of the situation that has unwantedly happened. Rather, it is acknowledging that if something has happened that conflicts with what matters to us, it makes sense for us to feel pain. Such acknowledgment allows us to no longer see the presence of the emotional pain as 'bad' but rather, a manifestation of our ability to care. This helps us to stop reacting to the feeling and instead to allow the itch to be there — in other words, to make room for the feeling.

Accepting uncomfortable emotions, such as anger, allows the discomfort to freely move. And more importantly, letting go of the struggle with discomfort further frees up our attention and actions; when we are no longer preoccupied with scratching the itch, we can more freely and wisely choose how to respond and what to bring our attention to.

However, this is not always easy to do — as explained, making room for emotional pain goes against our hardwiring. Therefore, emotional acceptance is an active process, requiring awareness and willingness.

Say 'okay' to the feeling

Responding consciously to discomfort firstly involves pausing and noticing when the emotion arises. It helps to take a deep breath. If we are feeling particularly overwhelmed (i.e. our stress response is triggered), it is important to engage in a focused grounding technique to activate our parasympathetic nervous system (the relaxation response), to help move our body out of flight, flight or freeze. For example, we can use the '333 rule' grounding technique:

Look around your environment and …

- name 3 things you can see

- name 3 sounds you can hear

- move 3 of your limbs (wriggle fingers and toes, rub palms together, roll your shoulders) or touch 3 objects around you.

Instead of becoming entangled in the mind's fight reaction, we can next simply notice and name the feeling. We then have space to notice what lies beneath the feeling, which allows us to acknowledge that it is okay to feel this way. Use these three steps to say to yourself:

'Hello [feeling].

You are there because I care about [your value].

And therefore, it's okay.'

> Hello [feeling]. You are there because I care about [value].
> And that's okay.

While you say the above, take a deep breath in. And lengthen the exhalation as you breathe out, giving a gentle sigh. With this breath, picture yourself creating space around the feeling, allowing what you care about to be there.

Once we have allowed the feeling to be there, we have space. This space gives us choice.

We may then choose to do nothing and shift our attention elsewhere. Or we may choose to act, respectfully; to take a stand and take action for what we believe and what matters to us. This does not mean trying to control the situation but instead attempting to influence the perceived injustice or wrongdoings, where we feel it is helpful and wise to do so.

Either way, whether we choose to act or not, the choosing process is conscious and guided by our values — what matters to us and the person we want to be — rather than being driven by the emotion, the mind's automatic narrative and the need to control the outcome. This conscious flexibility allows us to be aware of *how* we behave in what we decide to do. Even with the uncomfortable feeling inside us. Even with wrongdoing around us.

Accordingly, after naming and allowing the anger feeling, we can connect to our values by asking ourselves:

Who do I want to **be** in the world right now?

All together:

Hello [feeling]. You are here because I care about [your value]. And that's okay. Who do I want to be in the world right now?

These simple steps allow us to make room for emotional discomfort and connect to the integrity and wisdom in living our values, rather than suffering with the situation or feeling, which we cannot directly control. The practice can therefore take us from a state of disempowerment to re-empowerment in just a few short moments.

Re-empowering ourselves with emotional pain

In the story, when Wilbur reached into his pocket and found the daisy, still alive and graceful, he was reminded of what mattered to him. He was able to 'look' underneath his pain to reconnect to what was important to him. This realization opened space for Wilbur to make room for the anger he felt and to bring his attention back to his values — the person he wanted to be in the world. And for his values (e.g. to be neighbourly, calm and gracious) to guide his actions moving forward.

Wilbur reclaimed his sense of control and integrity by returning to his values, particularly with how he reapproached the unwanted situation next door. And ultimately, the spirit and vitality blossomed in him once again, even with the anger and unwanted issues still present.

Consciously choosing our behaviour in the presence of anger is extraordinarily freeing and empowering. It takes us back to what matters. To nurture who we truly want to be, and to choose to embody this even when life has not given us what we want. And just like Wilbur's garden returning to vitality, this allows us to keep flourishing. .

The Being Human method

The Being Human method brings together each process presented in the four books of the Being Human series. It is a method that involves four steps for awareness and connection. The first two steps — 'hello mind' and 'hello heart' — allow us to be aware of our humanness. The second two steps — 'hello being' and 'hello world' — allow us to connect to our beingness with ourselves, our fellow humans and the physical world.

You can practise just one step or the full method, in any moment. It is particularly helpful when you are experiencing psychological distress or unhelpful distraction/ disconnection.

1. Hello mind

a. Notice your thoughts — that is, what your mind is saying to you.

b. Identify whether these thoughts are a familiar 'story' that your mind has told you before. For example, your mind might be telling you thoughts around the 'I'm not good enough' story or the 'No one cares about me' story.

c. Ask yourself whether your thoughts are helping you right now.

'Hello mind. These thoughts are an old story.
They are not helping me right now.'

2. Hello heart

a. Name the feeling/sensations in your body.

b. Identify the value underneath the feeling — what is it that matters to you for this feeling to be there?

c. Allow the feeling/sensations to be there (without judging yourself or the feeling).

It can help to ground yourself by placing a hand on your heart and taking a slow, deep breath as you gently say to yourself:

> *'Hello heart. I am feeling [...]*
> *because I care about [value].*
> *And that's okay.'*

And now that you are connected to your values …

3. Hello being

Say hello to who you want to be in the world.

  a. Check in with your values (i.e. the person you want to be) in that moment.

  b. Choose a response/behaviour in alignment with your values.

Gently say to yourself:

> *'Hello being. Who do I want to be in the world right now?'*

4. Hello world

Say hello to the world around you. Reconnect to the physical world, including nature and people around you, by connecting with your senses.

Don't just see, but watch.

Don't just hear, but listen.

Don't just touch, but feel.

Don't just smell, but inhale.

Don't just taste, but savour.

And where appropriate, bring a 'wow' to that experience.

'Hello mind. Hello heart.
Hello being. Hello world.'

Resources

General resources

Baird, J. 2020, *Phosphorescence: On awe, wonder and things that sustain you when the world goes dark*, 4th Estate.

Brown, B. 2021, *Daring Greatly: How the courage to be vulnerable transforms the way we live, love, parent, and lead*, Penguin Life.

Carlson, R. 2017, *The Sense of Wonder: A celebration of nature for parents and children*, HarperCollins Publishers.

Coates, K. and Kolkka, S. 2022, *How to Be Well: A handbook for women*, Simon & Schuster.

Goodwin, K. 2023, *Dear Digital, We Need to Talk*: *A guilt-free guide to taming your tech habits and thriving in a distracted world*, Major Street Publishing.

Hari, J. 2022, *Stolen Focus: Why you can't pay attention*. Bloomsbury.

Johnson, S. 1999, *Who Moved My Cheese? An amazing way to deal with work and your life*, Vermilion.

Katie, B. 2018, *A Mind at Home with Itself: How asking four questions can free your mind, open your heart, and turn your world*, HarperOne.

Siegel, D. J. 2016, *Mind: A journey to the heart of being human*, W.W. Norton & Company.

Siegel, D, J. 2012, *Mindsight: The new science of personal transformation*, Bantam Books.

ACT resources

Eifert, G.H., McKay, M. and Forsyth, J.P. 2006, *ACT on Life Not on Anger: The new Acceptance & Commitment Therapy guide to problem anger*, New Harbinger Publications.

Harris, R. 2016, *The Single Most Powerful Technique for Extreme Fusion*, e-book, www.actmindfully.com.au/upimages/The_Single_Most_Powerful_Technique_for_Extreme_Fusion_-_Russ_Harris_-_October_2016.pdf

Harris, R. 2021, *The Happiness Trap: Stop struggling, start living*, 2nd edition. Exisle Publishing.

Hayes, L.L., Ciarrochi, J.V. and Bailey, A. 2022, *What Makes You Stronger: How to thrive in the face of change and uncertainty using Acceptance and Commitment Therapy*, New Harbinger.

Hayes, S. 2019, *A Liberated Mind: How to pivot toward what matters*, Avery.

Hayes, S.C. and Smith, S. 2005, *Get Out of Your Mind and Into Your Life: The new Acceptance and Commitment Therapy*, New Harbinger.

Leonard-Curtain, A. and Leonard-Curtain, T. 2019, *The power of small: How to make tiny but powerful changes when everything feels too much*, Hachette.

LeJeune, J. 'Pain and value: Two sides of the same coin', https://portlandpsychotherapy.com/2012/06/pain-and-values-two-sides-same-coin-0/

Oliver, J., Hill, J. and Morris, E. 2015, *Activate Your Life: Using acceptance and mindfulness to build a life that is rich, fulfilling and fun*, Constable & Robinson.

Acknowledgments

A heartfelt thank you to the team at Exisle Publishing for giving these books a welcoming home. A particular thank you to Gareth for seeing the potential in this series and to Anouska, Karen and Enni for taking such good care of these stories.

To the very talented Lizzie Szekely — I adore working with you and am constantly dazzled by your creative mind and your beautiful illustrations. Thank you for being so dedicated to these books and for befriending the 'W' characters the way you have.

I would like to thank Virginia Lloyd for her brilliance in editing the earlier versions of this series, and for her overall support in shaping this vision.

There were a number of friends and colleagues who generously gave their time to read initial manuscripts in this series and give their feedback: Kate James, Russ Harris, Aisling Curtain, Louise Hayes. I would also like to thank other folk within the ACBS community, for introducing me to ACT and for creating such a supportive community.

I am hugely grateful for my friends and family:

Warwick — for being a loyal cheerleader of this series. And of us.

Amber and Trinity — for your enthusiasm and support.

Ryan — for the time, care and wisdom you have given this series. Your way with the written word blows my mind.

My parents — Mum, Andrew, Dad and Chrissi — for your endless love, support, and for your devotion to your grandchildren.

Spencer, Alfie and Sullivan — you are my best little teachers of being attentive, curious and playful.

Thank you to all the human beings who have joined me in my therapy room — thank you for trusting me. Thank you for teaching me.

And finally, thank you to everyone who stepped into the first version of Winnie's world, and to those embarking on this Being Human series. I hope that reading the characters' stories helps you to normalise and choose compassion for our complex humanness, and to revel in our extraordinary world.

It really is so rare and beautiful that we even exist.